Working for our Future

Fighting Disease

Judith Anderson with Christian Aid

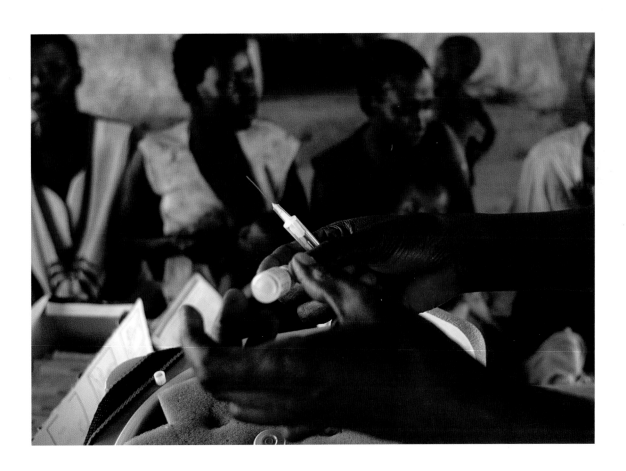

FRANKLIN WATTS
LONDON • SYDNEY

First published in 2007 by
Franklin Watts
338 Euston Road
London NW1 3BH

Franklin Watts Australia
Level 17/207 Kent Street
Sydney NSW 2000
Copyright © Franklin Watts 2007

Editor: Jeremy Smith
Art director: Jonathan Hair
Design: Rita Storey
Artwork: John Alston

Produced in association with Christian Aid.

Franklin Watts would like to thank Christian Aid for their help with this title, in particular for allowing permission to use the information concerning Maria and Marbella and Josué and Jaeli which is © Christian Aid. We would also like to thank the parents of Atkmatbek for the information and photographs provided.

Picture credits: Adrian Arbib/Christian Aid: 3br, 8t, 21 all, 27t. Alamy: 3, 6t, 9t, 13t, 14 all, 15t, 17tr, 18b, 20. Christian Aid/Sian Curry: 23 all, 24 all, 27b. Christian Aid/Annabel Davies: 3bl, 11, 12, 26b. Corbis: OFC, 4b, 10t, 16t, istockphoto.com: 4t, 5 all, 7 all, 8b, 13b, 15b, 28 all, 29b. Unicef: 3c, 25t, 29t. World Food Programme: 1, 18t, 19 all, 22b, 25r.

Dewey Classification 614.4

ISBN: 978 0 7496 7347 5

Printed in China

Franklin Watts is a division of Hachette Children's Books, an Hachette Livre UK company.

The Millennium Development Goals

In 2000, government leaders agreed on eight goals to help build a better, fairer world in the 21st century. These goals include getting rid of extreme poverty, fighting child mortality and disease, promoting education, gender equality and maternal health and ensuring sustainable development.

The aim of this series is to look at the problems these goals address, show how they are being tackled at local level and relate them to the experiences of children around the world.

Contents

Good health   4

No health care?   6

The problem of disease   8

HIV/AIDS   10

How does disease affect people? 12

Why are so many people affected? 14

The Millennium Development Goals 16

Government action   18

Local solutions   20

People who help   22

Protecting each other   24

A brighter future   26

Action you can take   28

Glossary/Find out more   30

Index   32

The Cast

Follow the stories of these children from around the world, all affected by disease in different ways.

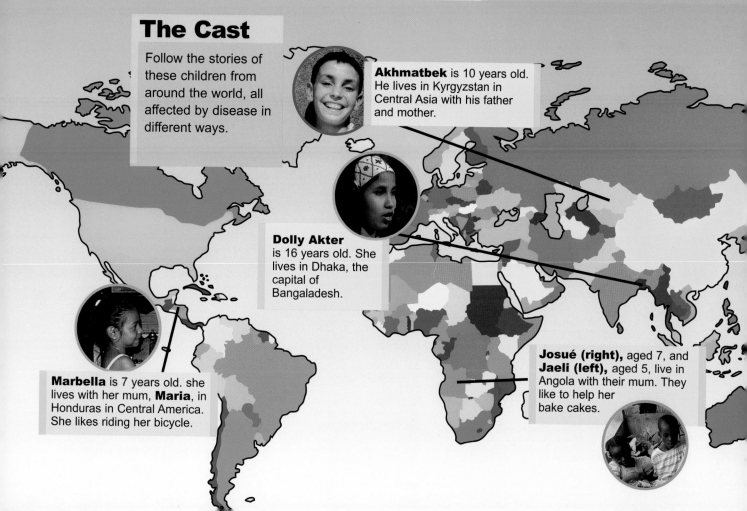

Akhmatbek is 10 years old. He lives in Kyrgyzstan in Central Asia with his father and mother.

Dolly Akter is 16 years old. She lives in Dhaka, the capital of Bangaladesh.

Marbella is 7 years old. she lives with her mum, **Maria**, in Honduras in Central America. She likes riding her bicycle.

Josué (right), aged 7, and **Jaeli (left),** aged 5, live in Angola with their mum. They like to help her bake cakes.

Good health

Do you feel well? Do you have lots of energy? Do you eat nutritious food, get a good night's sleep and take plenty of exercise? If you can answer yes to these questions, then you are probably very healthy. That's great!

▲ Plenty of fresh fruit and vegetables helps children grow strong and stay healthy. It gives them energy and helps them fight off illness.

Feeling ill

Good health is something we don't often think about until we feel ill. However, most of us suffer from colds, coughs or an upset tummy at some point. These common infections spread easily from person to person, making us feel poorly. We may lose our appetite, or have less energy for a day or two. Then we recover.

❝ When I had a bad cold I had to miss my friend's birthday party. ❞

Kelli, aged 10

◀ A common cold can spread quickly from person to person.

Getting better

If you are normally quite healthy, your body can fight off a mild infection such as a cold by itself. If the illness is more severe - flu perhaps, or an asthma attack or a bad stomach bug, then your doctor may give you some medicine to help you get better.

Fortunately, many of us live within travelling distance of a clinic or a hospital where we can get treatment whenever we need it. Most people in the developed world take good health and good health care for granted, but not everyone around the world can do this.

Raul, aged 8

" Last year nearly half the children in my class were sick at the same time. It was a tummy bug. My teacher was sick too. Then we got better. "

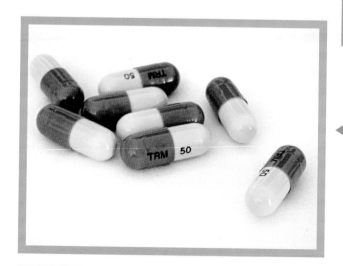

Medicines for many common illnesses can be bought over the counter at a chemist or drug store.

? What is the best thing about being healthy? Why is it important to eat well if you want to stay healthy?

No health care?

Some people do not have access to doctors, nurses, clinics or medicines. This may be because they cannot afford them, or it may be because there are no facilities where they live. If no one is sick, this isn't a problem. But what if someone is seriously ill? They might spread the illness to other people. They might die if they don't get treatment.

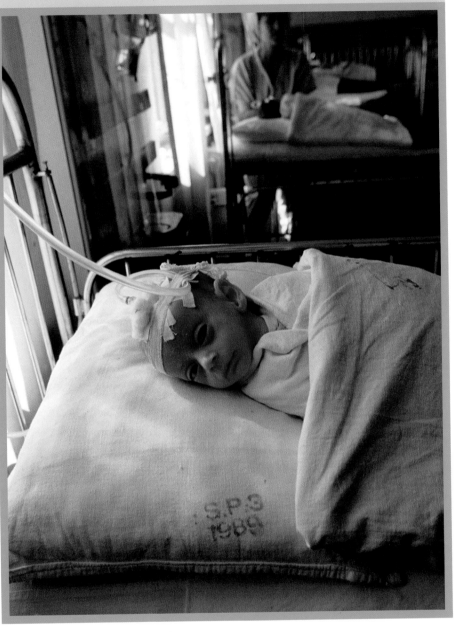

Common illnesses

Have you ever had an upset tummy? Sickness and diarrhoea are unpleasant, but it is extremely rare for someone who is usually healthy and well-fed to die from their effects. However, when someone is already weak from lack of food or water, such infections quickly become life threatening. In less developed countries with a shortage of basic medical care, diarrhoea kills millions of children every year.

This child is suffering from diarrhoea and malnutrition in the Intensive Care Unit at Tirana Childrens Hospital, Albania. Children are especially at risk from diarrhoea because they are not as strong as adults. Losing a lot of body fluid can be very dangerous for a child.

Immunisation

When you were a baby, you were probably given an injection or a drop on the tongue to protect you against various common diseases. This is known as immunisation. It means our bodies become immune to a particular type of infection. Not all disease can be prevented by immunisation, but some diseases have completely disappeared because of it, while other diseases such as polio and measles are much less common now. However, many people in less developed countries are not immunised. They continue to suffer from diseases that we know can be prevented.

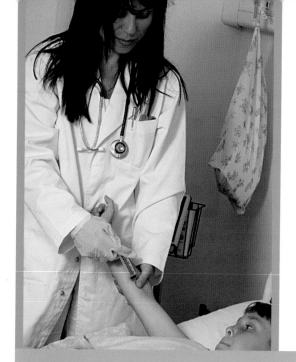

" A child can be immunised for $30 (£15). It is one of the simplest, most efficient, most cost effective ways of improving living standards on our planet. **"**

Statistic from the Global Alliance for Vaccines and Information.

" I've been immunised against tuberculosis. I had the injection when I was a baby. I can't remember it but I'm glad I've had it! **"**

Marianne, aged 9.

? **Have you been immunised against any diseases? If so, which ones?**

The problem of disease

An infectious disease is an illness that spreads from person to person. Not all disease is infectious. Heart disease, for example, cannot be caught from someone else. The problem with infectious diseases is that they can spread very quickly through the population, often with devastating results.

The spread of disease

People catch diseases in different ways. Some diseases such as flu and tuberculosis are spread by infected people coughing and sneezing. Diarrhoea is spread by drinking unclean food or water or contact with sewage because of poor sanitation. A serious disease called malaria is spread by a certain type of mosquito.

" Malaria comes when a mosquito bites you and then bad stuff from the mosquito gets inside you and then you're sick. "

Josué and his younger sister Jaeli live with their mum in Luanda, the capital city of Angola. Mosquitoes breed in the pools of stagnant water that collect in the streets after it rains. Recently, both children became very sick with malaria.

Not all mosquitoes spread malaria. The malarial mosquito (left) is found in hot countries and is mainly active at night.

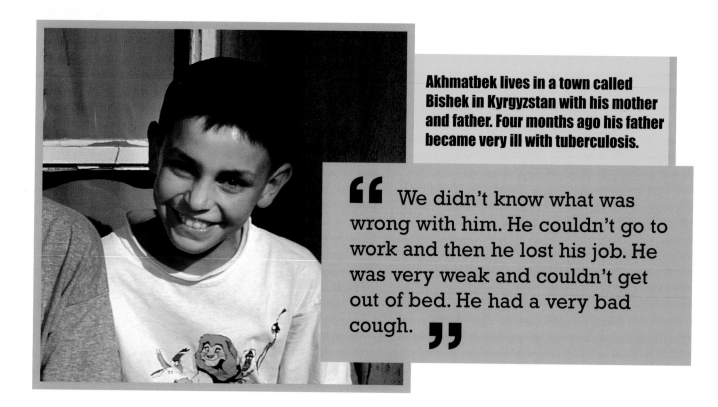

Akhmatbek lives in a town called Bishek in Kyrgyzstan with his mother and father. Four months ago his father became very ill with tuberculosis.

"We didn't know what was wrong with him. He couldn't go to work and then he lost his job. He was very weak and couldn't get out of bed. He had a very bad cough."

Around the world

Different diseases affect some parts of the world more than others. Diarrhoea is a particularly severe problem in countries where basic sanitation and clean water are hard to come by. Malaria affects people in hot countries where a particular type of mosquito is common. Tuberculosis is found all over the world, but affects poorer people most because they don't have access to a good diet and medicines to help them fight the disease.

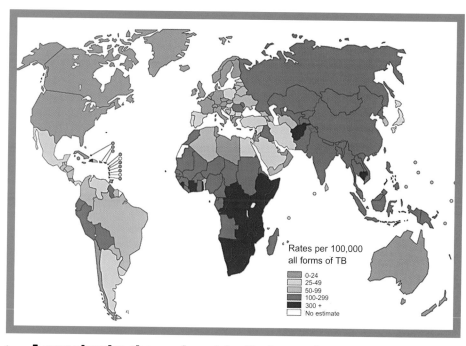

Rates per 100,000 all forms of TB

- 0-24
- 25-49
- 50-99
- 100-299
- 300 +
- No estimate

▲ A map showing the number of deaths from tuberculosis in 2003.

? **Akhmatbek lives in a single room with his parents. What do you think are his chances of becoming infected with tuberculosis?**

HIV/AIDS

You have probably heard of a disease called HIV/AIDS. At the moment there is no cure for this disease. Certain drugs help to delay the symptoms but they are very expensive. Another problem with HIV/AIDS is that many people do not know they are infected until after they have passed it on to others.

Estimated Number of AIDS-Related Deaths Worldwide, 1980-2000

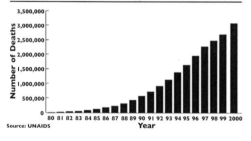

Source: UNAIDS

 A graph showing the rise in the number of deaths from AIDS between 1980-2000.

An estimated 15 million children around the world have lost one or both parents to HIV/AIDS. These children are in an orphanage in the Ukraine. Their parents died of HIV/AIDS.

What is HIV/AIDS?

AIDS is a disease caused by a virus called HIV. HIV is spread through infected blood (during a blood transfusion or an injection using a dirty needle) or by having unprotected sex. People may have HIV without knowing about it at first. However, when the disease takes hold their immune system (the body's natural defence against illness) breaks down and they are no longer healthy enough to fight off other illnesses. This is why many HIV/AIDS sufferers actually die of diseases such as tuberculosis and pneumonia that would be unlikely to kill somebody without the virus.

The effects on families

HIV/AIDS is particularly devastating to families, because the infection often passes between both parents, and can also pass from an expectant mother to her unborn child. The disease continues to grow steadily all around the world, creating families in which both parents have died and orphaned children have become the main carers for their young and often sick siblings.

" We found out that Marbella was infected when she was five years old. **"**

Maria Dolores talks about when she was told her daughter Marbella had the HIV virus. She was probably passed it by her mother before she was born.

? **How do you think Marbella's mum felt when she found out that Marbella has HIV?**

How does disease affect people?

If a serious infectious disease is left untreated, the infected person may die. Not only this, but they may spread the disease to other people while they are still alive. There are many other consequences too. A sick person cannot work or look after their family. They may have to rely on their children to care for them.

❝ When I found out that I was infected with HIV I felt as though the world had ended. I thought I was going to die soon and that I was going to leave my children as orphans. ❞

Marbella's mother Maria describes the terrible moment when she discovered she had the HIV virus.

Families

Because infectious disease spreads from person to person, whole families can become ill very quickly. When this happens, parents may be too unwell to look after sick children. Without a family member old enough or well enough to fetch water, prepare food, buy medicine, look after the farm or go to school, the future soon begins to look very bleak.

A chart from 2005 showing global deaths from four major diseases. ▶

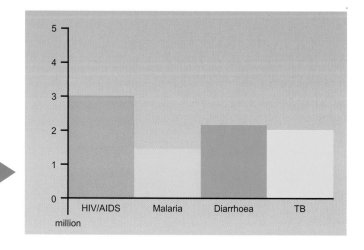

The cycle of poverty and disease

One of the biggest problems of disease is the poverty it creates. When someone is ill, they cannot work. They cannot grow food or earn a wage. They may become homeless, or they may find they cannot afford to eat properly or buy medicine. This means they are less likely to get better. They become trapped in a cycle of poverty and disease.

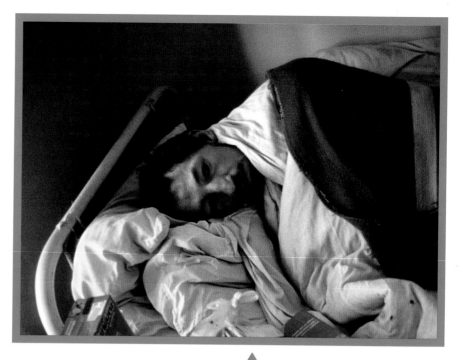

▲ Akhmatbek's father did not get the treatment he needed in the poorly equipped hospital in his country.

When Akhmatbek's father became ill with tuberculosis, he lost his job and the family couldn't afford to eat properly.

" Mum said that Dad needed soup. But we only had bread and tea. "

? **What would help to break the cycle of poverty and disease in Akhmatbek's family?**

Why are so many people affected?

Many infectious diseases are either preventable, or curable. Yet in Africa, a child dies of malaria every ten seconds. Around the world, someone dies of tuberculosis every 15 seconds, and over 40 million people worldwide are now infected with HIV/AIDS. Why is this happening?

▲ A typical slum in Dhaka, Bangladesh, with open, dirty water flowing through. One in six of the world's population have to drink unsafe water every day.

Poverty

One of the main reasons for the continued growth in infectious disease is poverty. Poverty means people cannot afford to eat well and have access to good sanitation and clean water. Poverty means people cannot afford immunisations, medicines and doctors' fees. Poverty means people live in cramped and overcrowded housing where disease spreads even faster.

" Millions of children have died from malaria because they were not protected by an insecticide-treated bed net or did not receive effective treatment. We can stop this tragedy. **"**

Bill Gates, Chairman of Microsoft and the Bill Gates Foundation which helps poorer countries to fight disease through donations.

Lack of information

Nevertheless, some methods of preventing the spread of disease are cheap and simple. An inexpensive mosquito net over a child's bed at night will protect them from malaria, while information on basic hygiene can stop the spread of diseases such as diarrhoea and tuberculosis. But how do people in remote or poorer areas receive this information? Teachers have to be trained and paid for. It all comes back to money.

" South Africa's Malaria Control Program has been quite successful in establishing procedures for mosquito control; looking to educate people in at-risk areas. "

Eugene Brantly, Malaria Progamme Director at a research institute called RTI International speaks about the success of its education programme in South Africa. It delivers malaria help to more than 600,000 South Africans.

डी. डी. टी. छिड़काव से मलेरिया मिटाइये

ERADICATE MALARIA BY SPRAYING

An Indian poster from 2006 instructing people how stop malaria spreading.

? **What would you do to make sure that everyone learns how to prevent the spread of diseases like malaria?**

The Millennium Development Goals

Many diseases are preventable, yet because of poverty and lack of education millions of people continue to be infected every year. In the year 2000, the world's leaders met and agreed a set of eight goals that would help to make the world a better, fairer place in the 21st century. All eight goals are connected and in order to achieve them, every single country, rich and poor, needs to work together and play a part.

French President Chirac (right) welcomes UN Secretary-General Kofi Annan and former British prime minister Tony Blair at the Elysee Palace to discuss the Millennium Development Goals in 2003.

The Goals

All eight goals have targets that need to be reached by the year 2015 and governments have been asked to make policies to ensure these targets are met. The target for fighting disease is to stop the spread of malaria, tuberculosis and HIV/AIDS by 2015. This can only be achieved through the success of prevention programmes as well as treatment programmes. It requires a huge commitment from every single country in the world.

1 Get rid of extreme poverty and hunger

2 Primary education for all

3 Promote equal chances for girls and women

4 Reduce child mortality

5 Improve the health of mothers

6 Combat HIV/AIDS, malaria and other diseases

7 Ensure environmental sustainability

8 Address the special needs of developing countries, including debt and fair trade

NO EXCUSE 2015

MILLENNIUM CAMPAIGN

A spokesperson for the Millennium Campaign (logo shown left).

MA TÚY AIDS

KHÔNG ĐƯỢC THỬ DÙ CHỈ MỘT LẦN

A poster educating the public about AIDS in Hanoi, Vietnam.

> " We need everyone's voice to join together and demand that governments live up to their promises to achieve the Millennium Development Goals by 2015. "

A global concern

The problem of HIV/AIDS and other diseases are not just a problem for countries in the developing world. Under the commitments made in the Millennium Development Goals, world leaders agreed to push drugs companies to make vaccines and treatments for deadly diseases available to everyone in the world – not just those people who can afford them. With people moving from developing countries moving to other places, it is also vital to help these people stay disease free in order to stop such illnesses spreading further across the globe.

A leaflet about HIV/AIDS in Zambia says:

> " It's my problem.
>
> It's your problem.
>
> It's our problem.
>
> So what are you going to do about it? "

? **Leaflets like the one on HIV/AIDS help raise awareness about disease. But many people in developing countries cannot read. How can these people be given the information they need?**

Government action

Disease is a global problem. It has the potential to affect every single one of us. So halting and reversing the spread of the most serious infectious diseases requires a global response. All countries and governments need to work together to bring about change and ensure a healthier world.

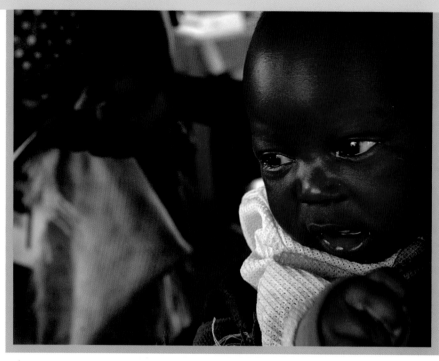

 A young child receiving a vaccination for polio in Addis-Ababa, Ethiopia.

 A poorly facilitated hospital in Lagos, Nigeria.

What governments can do

Governments of poorer, less economically developed countries can put people first by training more doctors and nurses, building more clinics and hospitals and providing medicines and immunisation programmes. They can also teach people how to prevent disease through simple measures such as better hygiene.

Sharing the cost

Governments of richer, more economically developed countries can provide financial help so that more health services are available to poorer people who are often at most risk from disease. They can invest in research to develop new medicines and immunisations. They can also reduce the cost of expensive drugs and equipment that poorer countries need and make sure that these treatments are readily available.

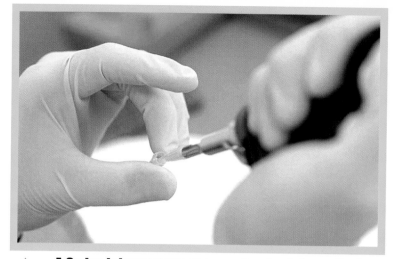

A Swiss laboratory test a vaccine for tuberculosis. Making this affordable for poorer countries drastically cuts the death rate from the disease.

Success stories

Some global responses are already having an effect. The World Health Organisation has developed a special programme known as DOTS to help combat tuberculosis. In countries that have committed themselves to this programme, the number of cases being detected and cured has risen sharply.

This mother from Afghanistan had tuberculosis. She is now better and able to look after her family because of the joint efforts of the World Health Organisation and the World Food Programme who gave her the medicines she needed.

? **Why is it particularly important that all countries work together to stop the spread of disease?**

Local solutions

Governments must work together to make new policies and provide more money in the fight against disease. However, much of the vital work of immunizing children and running clinics and health education programmes is carried out by charities and aid organizations who can respond quickly to the needs of local communities.

Fighting tuberculosis in Kyrgyzstan

Akhmatbet's father was very ill at first, but because he lost his job he could not afford to stay in hospital. Then a nurse from the local branch of the Red Crescent Society began to visit him at home every day. She made sure he received the medicine he needed, checked on his progress and even brought food for the family. Now he is well enough to go to the Red Crescent canteen each day where he is given his medicine and a hot meal. Nurse Svetlana Sooronova of the Kyrgyz Red Crescent Society says that many of the people she treats do not have the money to get to a hospital or doctor, and are rejected by their relatives for fear of infection. She says these people rely totally on the Red Crescent Society.

❝ I like the nurses. They made my father better and now he plays chess with me again. **❞**

Akhmatbek

Jaeli (far left) and Josué (quoted below) were nursed back to health by their mother, Tabita (below).

66 We were sick, I was hot. Mummy looked after me and gave me medicine. Then I was better. 99

Combating sickness in Angola

In Angola, the Evangelical Congregational Church (IECA) runs a project to teach poorer women about health and hygiene. The project is based in Luanda, the capital city, where malaria and diarrhoea are very common. The IECA taught Josué and Jaeli's mum Tabita how to treat various types of sickness. This meant that when her children became ill, she knew what to do.

? **What do you think might have happened to Akhmatbek's father if he had not been visited by a nurse from the Red Crescent Society?**

People who help

People from all over the world are helping to fight disease. Doctors, nurses and teachers travel to local communities to set up clinics, immunise children and provide information about how to stay healthy. Scientists work to develop new and better medicines, while fundraisers work to raise money for projects such as improving a water supply.

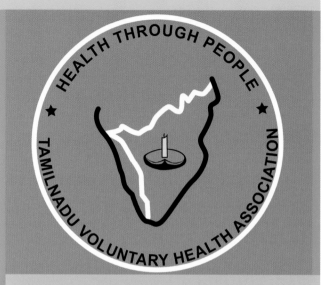

Miss Girja, a worker for the Tamil Nadu Voluntary Health Association (logo above), describes her reasons for wanting to join the organisation.

" I was keen to work directly with the community and felt that being a counsellor would enable me to have this contact. I am often inspired by the determination and calm manner in which some of the patients I counsel deal with their illnesses. **"**

Inspired by others

Counsellors are people trained to offer support and advice to those suffering from diseases such as tuberculosis and HIV/AIDS. Miss Girja trained as a counsellor for Tamil Nadu Voluntary Health Association in India. Canadian Red Cross worker Richard McCabe helps to provide health promotion, education and prevention advice.

◀ **Canadian Red Cross worker Richard McCabe visits families with health problems in Nicaragua.**

Spreading the word

Francisco, aged 18, and Nelson, aged 16, live in Angola. They have both been specially trained to teach students at their school about how to prevent the spread of HIV/AIDS and malaria.

Nelson (right)

" We tell people how the diseases are transmitted and explain how you can avoid getting sick. We need to do this so that people know how to stay healthy. I've had malaria, and so have other people in my family but thankfully we all got better. **"**

Francisco (above)

" We do workshops at school and in the community. For example, we tell them that stagnant water is a breeding ground for mosquitoes, and we show people how to kill mosquitoes with insect spray. It's a very good thing to be involved in. Everybody needs to know about malaria and HIV/AIDS, because lots of people get sick and die from these diseases. **"**

? **Why are Francisco and Nelson so keen to help prevent the spread of HIV/AIDS and malaria?**

Protecting each other

One of the most effective ways of fighting disease is to prevent people getting sick in the first place. Malaria can be avoided if people learn to take precautions to protect themselves and their families. Tuberculosis can be prevented through immunisation. Diarrhoea can be reduced if people have access to clean water and teach each other about better hygiene.

This lady in Angola has set up a stall outside a maternity hospital. She hands out free mosquito nets to expectant mothers, because babies are especially at risk from malaria.

No more malaria

Mosquitoes that carry the malaria infection are mainly active at night. The best way for people to protect each other is to use devices that stop the mosquitoes from reaching you in the first place. Sleeping under a mosquito net or spraying a room with insecticide are all cheap, effective ways of reducing the threat. Local groups in centres such as Angola are putting these measures into practise.

Emilia Nakaué is the head of a small group of volunteers in Angola that have trained in malaria and HIV awareness. Since Emilia found out about mosquito nets (shown right of picture), everyone sleeps under them, and none of her three younger children have had the disease.

Reducing diarrhoea

Dolly Akter, aged 16, lives in a slum neighbourhood of Dhaka, the capital of Bangladesh. She is involved in a UNICEF project to improve sanitation and hygiene in her area. She and her friends go from house to house, making sure that people understand the importance of washing and using only clean, covered water.

A water sanitation system set up by French firemen provides clean water for all the residents of this camp in Indonesia.

> **Before it was such a dirty and undeveloped area. Nowadays it is different. The children in our area don't get diarrhoea so often, and they laugh and play more now that they are healthier.**

Dolly Akter talks about the changes in her neighbourhood in Bangladesh.

? **Dolly visits her neighbours to tell them about good hygiene. What else can be done to reduce the spread of diarrhoea in slum areas?**

A brighter future

Fighting disease means many different things. It means preventing the spread of disease by taking protective measures. It means developing better medicines and treating those who are already suffering from disease. It also means fighting one of the principle causes of disease – poverty – so that everyone has a chance of a brighter, healthier future.

Building hope

When Maria Dolores discovered that she and her daughter Marbella were infected with HIV, she didn't know what to do. Their health suffered and she lost all hope. Then she found out about an association of self-help groups for people with HIV/AIDS. She started to attend workshops to learn about her illness and how she could help herself and Marbella. Now she runs a group of her own.

Maria speaks about the work of the group. Everyone helps everybody else out.

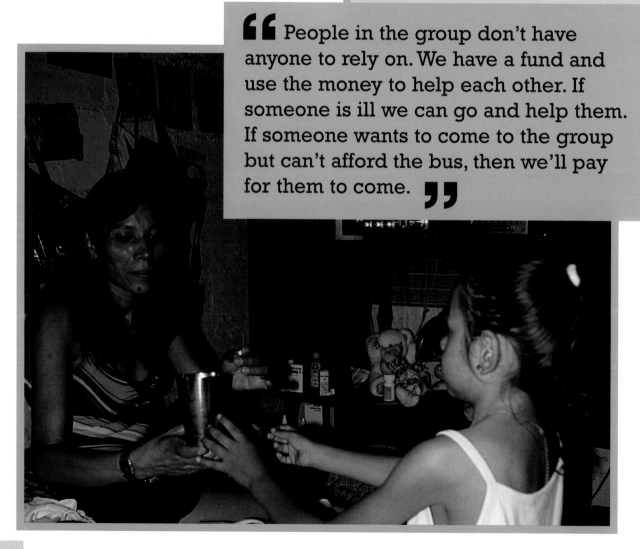

❝ People in the group don't have anyone to rely on. We have a fund and use the money to help each other. If someone is ill we can go and help them. If someone wants to come to the group but can't afford the bus, then we'll pay for them to come. **❞**

Happy and well

When Josué and Jaeli's mum Tabita went to classes at the IECA centre, she didn't only learn about how to prevent and treat malaria. She also learnt to cook! Now she supports the family by baking cakes and selling them. She can afford to send Josué and Jaeli to school.

❝ I mix the eggs and the cake in the bowl. I like eating the cakes. I like the Christmas tree cake best! ❞

Tabita describes how she enjoys cooking for her family, especially treats such as cakes.

Dolly Akhter's parents are very clear about the advantages of her training in health and hygiene.

❝ Dolly learns more, then our family learns more. We don't get diarrhoea any more. Our family always knows about hygiene and being clean, so we don't get sick. ❞

? How has educating people like Dolly helped other members of her community?

Action you can take

Disease causes terrible suffering, prevents people from working and hinders the development of whole countries. It keeps families in poverty and stops children from getting the education they need. Yet if everyone works together, the spread of disease can be halted and even reversed.

Write a postcard to the leader of your country demanding that they keep the promises made in the Millennium Development Goals.

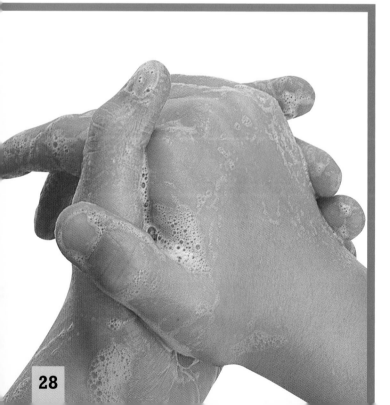

Make sure you wash your hands after using the toilet to avoid spreading germs.

Write to your government

The problem of disease is greatest in developing countries. Yet there are many things we can do to help those who may seem far away. Campaign for change by writing to your government representative and asking them to uphold the promises enshrined in the Millennium Development Goals.

Take care of yourself

Fighting the spread of disease is the responsibility of every single one of us. The first thing we can do is make sure that we are not spreading disease ourselves. Washing hands, using clean water, eating healthy food and getting immunised against diseases such as tuberculosis, polio and measles help us to stay healthy. They also mean that we are not putting those around us at risk.

Hold an awareness assembly

Research a particular problem such as diarrhoea in a remote village without access to clean water. Then hold an assembly at your school, using words, pictures and perhaps a short play to raise awareness about the issues.

Join an action group

There are hundreds of charities and action groups that raise money for medicines, equipment and clinics in the developing world. Many have special youth programmes or posters or websites to raise awareness and tell you about specific things you can do to help. Check out charities such as Save the Children, UNICEF, The International Red Crescent and Red Cross, WaterAid and Health Unlimited. Or set up one of your own!

Join a charity or action group such as UNICEF (right).

Raise money

Hold a cake sale, do a sponsored run or swim, offer a hair braiding or shoe shining service, wash cars, put on a play or concert. There are so many ways to raise money for your chosen charity – the more inventive, the better!

Think of a way to raise money for a charity, such as doing a sponsered swim.

? How will you help to improve the lives of children like Akhmatbek, Dolly, Marbella, Josué and Jaeli?

Glossary

Charity an organisation that uses money donated by members of the public to help others

Diarrhoea an illness spread by dirty food and water or not washing hands after going to the toilet

HIV/AIDS a disease which attacks the body's natural immune system

Hygiene keeping clean

Immunisation an injection or medicine that protects us from a particular disease

Infection an illness or disease that we pick up from our environment

Insecticide chemicals which kill insects such as mosquitoes

Malaria a dangerous disease spread by a type of mosquito that lives in hot, humid climates

Measles a common childhood illness; it kills many children each year in countries which do not immunise against it

Millennium Development Goals (MDGs) 8 goals agreed by world leaders in the year 2000 with the aim of eradicating poverty and disease and promoting the rights of disadvantaged people

Mortality death

Nutritious healthy food, good for growth and energy

Polio a disease which affects the spinal chord; immunisation programmes mean that polio has completely disappeared from many parts of the world

Sanitation drains for dirty water and waste from toilets

Stagnant water water that is no longer fresh; dirty water

Tuberculosis a serious lung infection

United Nations an organisation of countries from all around the world with the aim of promoting peace, development and human rights

Virus a type of disease which spreads from one person to another

Find out more

Useful websites

www.cyberschoolbus.un.org/mdgs
This site introduces all eight Millennium Development Goals with facts, photos and video clips to illustrate each one.

Send your story or poem about how any of the issues in this book have affected you to: **addyourvoice@unorg** and view stories from other children on the link above (go to "Add your voice").

www.millenniumcampaign.org/goals
The official site for the latest news on the Millennium Development Goals. Click on "Goal 6" to find the latest developments, facts and statistics as well as information about what you can do in the fight against diseases such as malaria and HIV/AIDS.

www.millenniumcampaign.org
Click on "Who's Doing What" (top of page) then "Youth", and download the Youth Action Guide.

www.unicef.org/voy/explore/wes/explore
Click on "Brainteasers" 2 and 3 for interesting facts and pictures about the links between water and health. Go to "Keep it clean!" to find out how to protect yourself and others against diarrhoea.

www.wateraid.org.uk/international/ learn_zone/4967.asp
Watch a short film about the need for clean, safe drinking water around the world.

www.kidshealth.org/kid/health_problems/ infection/hiv.html
A website all about HIV/AIDS - what it is and how it affects people.

www.ifrc.org
Official website of the Red Cross/Red Crescent organisation.

Christian Aid websites

Christian Aid contributed two of the real-life stories in this book (the accounts of Josué and Jaeli, and Marbella and Maria). You can find out more about this organisation by following the links below:

www.christian-aid.org.uk
The main site for the charity Christian Aid, who help out disadvantaged children and adults all over the world, regardless of their religion.

www.globalgang.org.uk
Christian Aid's website for kids with games, news and stories from around the world.

Index

action, taking 28-29
Afghanistan 19, 22
Angola 8, 21, 23, 24

Bangladesh 14, 25

charities 20-21, 29, 30
Chirac, Jacques 16
countries
        developing 16, 17, 28, 29
less developed 6, 7, 18
more developed 19, 30
counsellors 22

diarrhoea 6, 8, 9, 15, 21, 24, 25, 27, 29
disease
        effects of 12-13
infectious 4, 8-9, 12, 14, 18
prevention of 7, 14, 15, 16, 24-25, 26, 28
spread of 6, 8-9, 10, 11, 12, 14, 15, 18,
        23, 26
doctors 5, 6, 14, 18, 20, 22

education 15, 16, 17, 21, 22, 23, 25, 27
Ethiopia 18

Gates, Bill 14
Geldof, Bob 16

health, maintaining 4-5, 28
HIV/AIDS 10-11, 12, 14, 16, 17, 22, 23,
        26, 30
Honduras 11
hygiene 15, 18, 21, 24, 25, 27
immunisations 7, 14, 18, 19, 20, 22,
        24, 28

IECA 21, 27
India 22

Kyrgyzstan 9, 20

malaria 8-9, 14, 15, 16, 21, 23, 24, 27
malnutrition 6, 30
measles 7, 28
medicines 5, 6, 9, 12, 13, 14, 18, 19,
        20, 21
developing 19, 22, 26
Millenium Development Goals 16-17, 28,
        30, 31
mosquitoes 8, 9, 23, 24

Nigeria 18
nurses 5, 6, 18, 22

orphans 10, 11, 12
organisations, aid 20

polio 7, 18, 28
poverty 13, 14, 16, 26, 28, 30

Red Crescent Society 20, 21, 29

Tamil Nadu Voluntary Health Association
        22
tuberculosis 7, 8, 9, 10, 13, 14, 15, 16,
19, 20, 22, 24, 28

Ukraine 10
UNICEF 25, 29, 30

Vietnam 17
virus 10, 11

World Health Organisation 12, 19

Zambia 17